D0927902

Thorsons
An Imprint of HarperCollinsPublishers
77–85 Fulham Palace Road
Hammersmith, London W6 8JB
1160 Battery Street,
San Francisco, California 94111–1213

First published in France by Éditions Fontaine 1995
Thorsons edition 1996

10 9 8 7 6 5 4 3 2 1

English edition © Thorsons 1996
English translation by Lisa Eaton

A catalogue record for this book
is available from the British Library

ISBN 0 7225 3381 0

Printed in France

The Kama Sutra in 3D

Illustrations by François Guérin

Text adaptation by Martine Dorra

Thorsons

An Imprint of HarperCollins*Publishers*

Happy are the lands whose gods make love...
Étiemble

I It was Sir Richard Burton (1821–1890), the great scholar and explorer, who first introduced the Kama Sutra to a European audience. Written in Sanskrit by Vatsyayana between the second and sixth centuries, the Kama Sutra – 'Aphorisms on Love' – is a great work in the Indian tradition for which love is an art, a sensual pleasure, a means of touching the divine.

For in the beginning there were two...
Secluded in the Himalayas after the suicide of his wife Sati, Shiva was deep in meditation. The beautiful Parvati, reincarnation of Sati, stood close by him, but the god seemed unaware of her presence. Meanwhile, the world was on the road to ruin, threatened by the evil spirit Takara. One hero alone, descended from the seed of Shiva, could overcome the evil. But how was he to do this? The gods appealed to Kama. After a few million years, Kama shot an arrow which hit Shiva right in the middle of his forehead. Furious at being disturbed in his meditation, Shiva reduced Kama to ashes. Discovering Parvati, Shiva admired her patience and offered to grant her a wish. 'That Kama lives and warms the world. Without Kama, I desire nothing.' Shiva duly consented. So Kama lived, but ananga, without a body. Shiva and Parvati had a son, Kumara, who did indeed kill the demon. This ancient god Kama possessed a bow of sugar cane and an arrow of flowers, which, like Eros, he fired at humans. Thus Kama is love, pleasure, sensual delight of the five senses, amorous desire, yet also all forms of desire.

Together with Artha, worldly wealth and power, and Dharma, religious merit, Kama is one of the three 'principles' of human existence. They are crowned by a transcendent finality, Moksha, deliverance, dispenser of reincarnation.

Composed of seven parts, the Kama Sutra deals with the achievement of Kama. Only the second part relates to the act of sexual union. The author Vatsyayana, with a constant concern for feminine pleasure, explains in great detail the different embraces, kisses, scratches, bites, blows and sounds which this pleasure brings; the various positions; the art of making the most skilful use of the lingam, the male organ, and the yoni, the female organ; as well as the practices of the eunuchs. In the rest of the book, Vatsyayana describes the relations a man should have with his wives and those of others, the women he is entitled to seduce, and the formulas for success in these challenges (aphrodisiacs, magic, accessories...). He also lavishes his advice on skilled and respected courtesans. He incites men and women to study the 'sixty-four arts', which include chemistry, the trick of musical glasses filled with water, architecture, how to teach parrots to talk...
Amusing, light-hearted and mischievous, this manual of how to live and how to love draws us in to the life of the privileged few whom Vatsyayana chooses to address.

May this playful interpretation of the Kama Sutra set you dreaming!
Martine Dorra

HOW TO LOOK AT THESE IMAGES

Technique 1 — Look in the direction of the image but without focusing on an exact point. Let your gaze drift into this space and relax. After a few moments you will 'sense' that something is happening. A transformation will begin to take place in the design; continue your relaxed gaze. Your eyes will do all the work; you just need to be patient. The emergence of the three-dimensional image will generally begin with one part. Carry on looking into the distance without focusing and the rest of the picture will emerge in full 3D.

Technique 2 — Place the illustration at the end of your nose. The design should blur completely. Give your eyes time to get used to it and then, without changing the focus of your eyes, move it away slowly. Stop when your arms are extended – the design will probably be blurred: in this case, relax; if not, repeat the process. After several attempts, this should no longer be difficult. There are several ways of seeing images in 3D, but the key to their success lies in not focusing hard on the image and keeping it hazy. If the image doesn't appear at the first attempt, don't worry – you are not alone. The first time you try to see the image, don't keep working at it or you will put your eyes through gymnastics which they are not used to and risk straining them. Try again a little later.

Technique 3 — This method is called the method of 'seeing through the mirror'. You do this by fixing your gaze behind the virtual image. In the course of this process, the image will begin to lose its clarity and your eyes will automatically adapt. As with the other techniques, stay relaxed. Once you are used to exploring these pictures like this, this technique will probably prove to be the quickest for seeing the inner image in 3D.

HOW YOUR EYES WILL SEE THE IMAGE

A ll the illustrations in this book have been designed to be seen through the mirror. Once you are familiar with this stereoscopic visualization, train yourself to look at them with a squint or while going slightly cross-eyed. It takes time to learn this technique, but it will give you a reversed vision of the inner image. Here is a diagram:

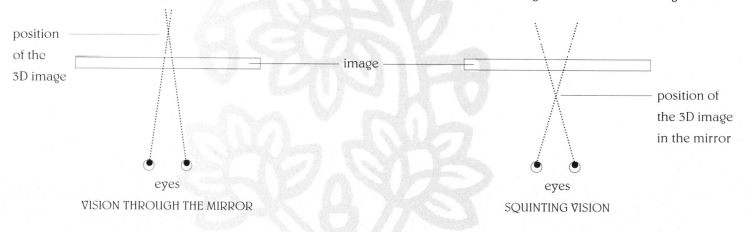

position of the 3D image

image

position of the 3D image in the mirror

eyes

eyes

VISION THROUGH THE MIRROR

SQUINTING VISION

E xperienced readers will be able to put this technique to the test if they find it easy to see all the images in this book. Once you have found one three-dimensional image, you should be able to find other 3D pictures. To do this, allow the 3D image to appear. Then, find inside this image a wide, flat surface. Train yourself to make it hazy with the help of one of the methods described. Be patient – this technique requires greater concentration and it will seem as if you are starting from scratch. A modified version of the first picture will appear, and you will be captivated by a second image; in fact, some people can even find a third picture. This seems more difficult, however, if not impossible with images which do not offer a wide, flat surface. And don't forget: avoid relentless effort – this technique is even more demanding on your eye muscles.

THE PRELUDES

A
Ardent young men, do not neglect the preliminaries!

Endeavour to satisfy your mistress. Listen to her desires.

Some men, carried away by the power of their desire, forget the prelude,

only to be surprised when they are pushed away later! Yet it is such a delight to

kiss, to caress, to nibble one another…To explore with your hand or

your mouth her body, her breasts, her neck, her belly, down to her

innermost curves. Fulfilled, the beloved shall return these kisses and

caresses wholeheartedly. No part of the beloved's body should be neglected.

Her lover shall make it his duty to discover them, to reveal to his mistress

all the pleasure she can receive from them.

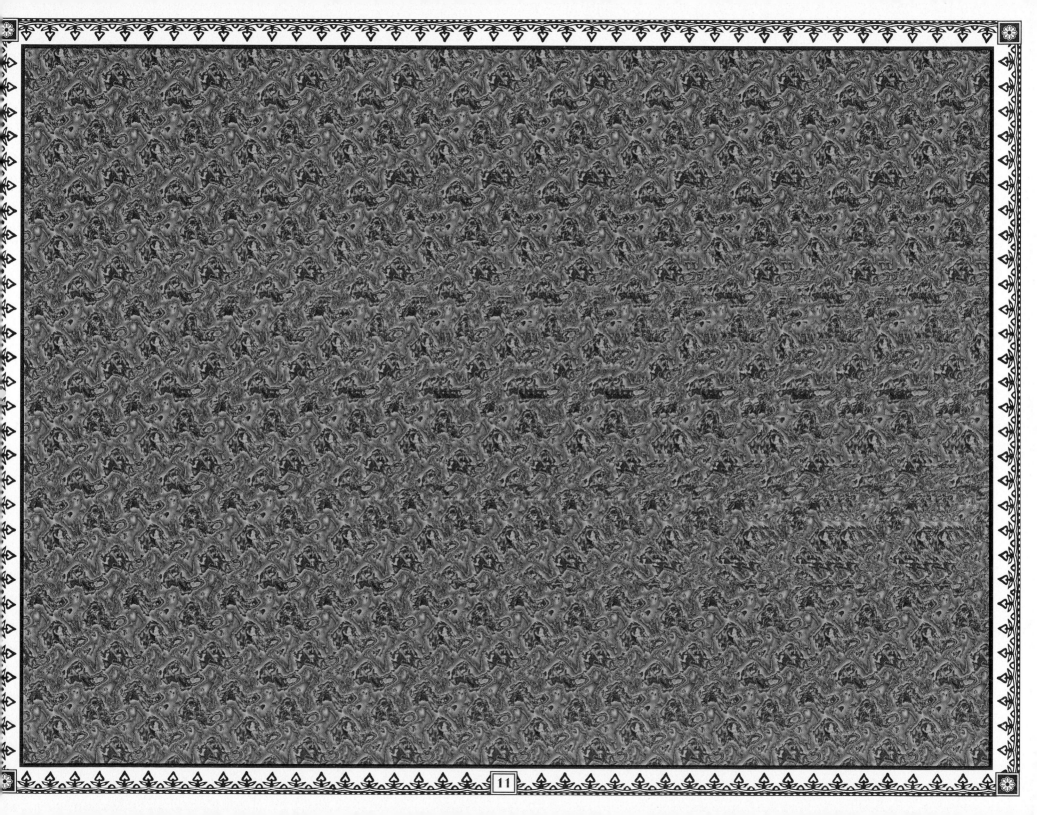

THE YAWNING

A pale moon shines down on the sleeping beauty. Kneeling beside her, the lover wakes her with a kiss on her modest brow. Keeping her eyelids lowered, she smiles. Grasping her rounded hips, the lover slides her onto his knees. The beauty raises her legs, widely spread. Her ankle bracelets ring out joyously. The lover, eager, wants to possess what the beauty reveals to him. The tease shies away, the lover protests. To silence him, the beauty places her plump foot on his mouth. One by one, the lover kisses her pearly nails, nibbles her little toes. The beauty coos. She coos so loudly that she wakes the dove. The bird, alarmed, responds. The beauty laughs. Taking advantage of her distraction, with one ingenious move, the lover slides into the coveted yoni.

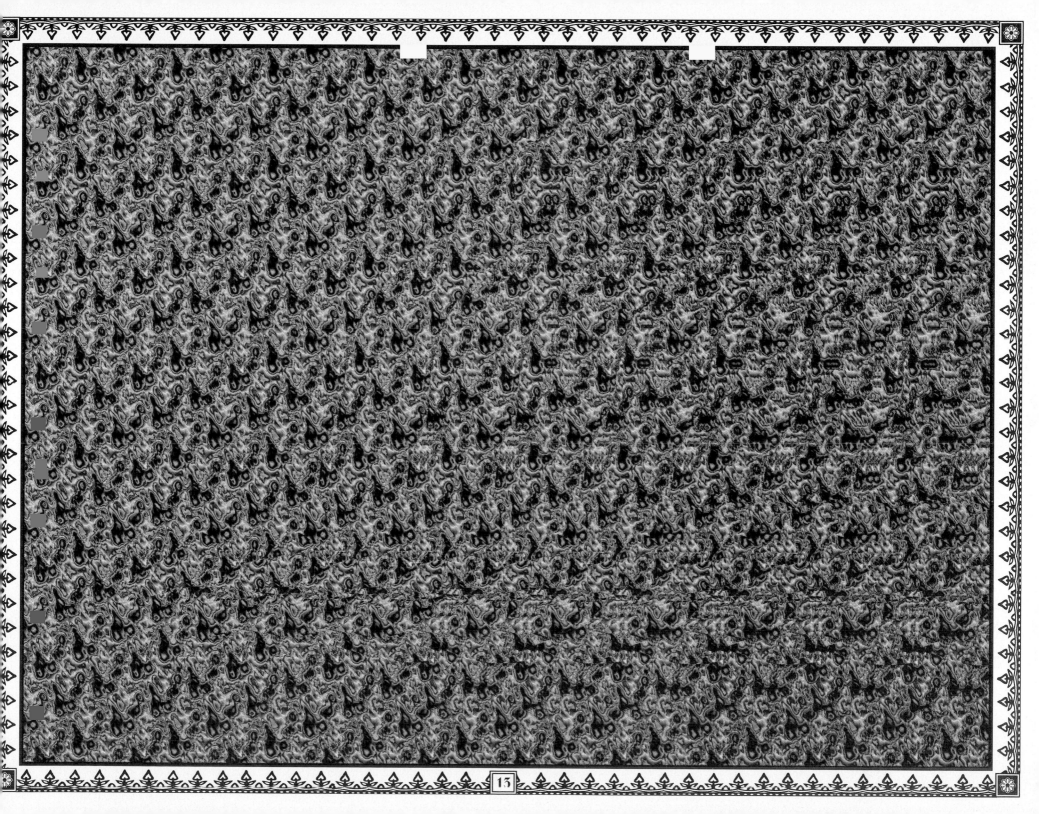

THE COBRA

He is a perfect man, educated, rich and respected by all.

Only his wife knows his weakness. Valiant and skilful at all sorts of games,

he lacks vigour in those of love. So she gives him potions to drink, milk mixed

with sugar, uchchata root, pepper and liquorice. Or rice with sparrow's eggs.

She covers herself with perfumed unguents and oils and, with skilful caresses,

awakens the lazy lingam. Erect from her kisses, it is eventually ready to act.

Then, like a snake, the beauty turns around, slithers and coils up among

the cushions. The husband did not expect this reversal of the situation.

He is all excited now. Blindly, his lingam searches for the yoni.

It is the coupling of the cobra.

THE CONCH

Sea-woman, her hair soaked with sweat, coils up like seaweed around her lover's arms. Siren-woman, her teeth have the same lustre as the pearls adorning her neck. He, the fisherman, tries to grasp the pink tongue between his lips, but it flees quickly like a small fish. He holds his breath and dives towards the yoni and its holy glints. A cruel bite draws a cry from him. She does not let her prey go, the moray eel! Octopus-woman, she enlaces the fisherman and drags him down to the bottom of the abyss. Joyously, he lets himself drown…Eventually, the beauty surrenders. He then climbs astride her lifted thighs and mounts her, keeping her firmly in position under his knees. In the ocean of pleasures, they are the two united valves of a beautiful shellfish: the conch.

THE SWING

He is a man of taste. In his garden there are two swings,

one revolving and one ordinary. He spends many pleasant moments there,

conversing with his friends. Sometimes, alone, he switches from one to the other

until his head spins. But his favourite swing has neither ropes, nor wood, nor cushions.

He finds it with his favourite mistress, a skilful and passionate courtesan.

Adorned with pearls and gold, a simple veil of silk hiding her nudity, she stretches out

her arms towards him. The night will be long…They revisit each of the

sixty-four chapters. And, to finish, the swing. She sits on his lap, her legs raised.

With one hand, he holds her, with the other, he caresses her breasts. She swings back

and forth, faster and faster, until bliss.

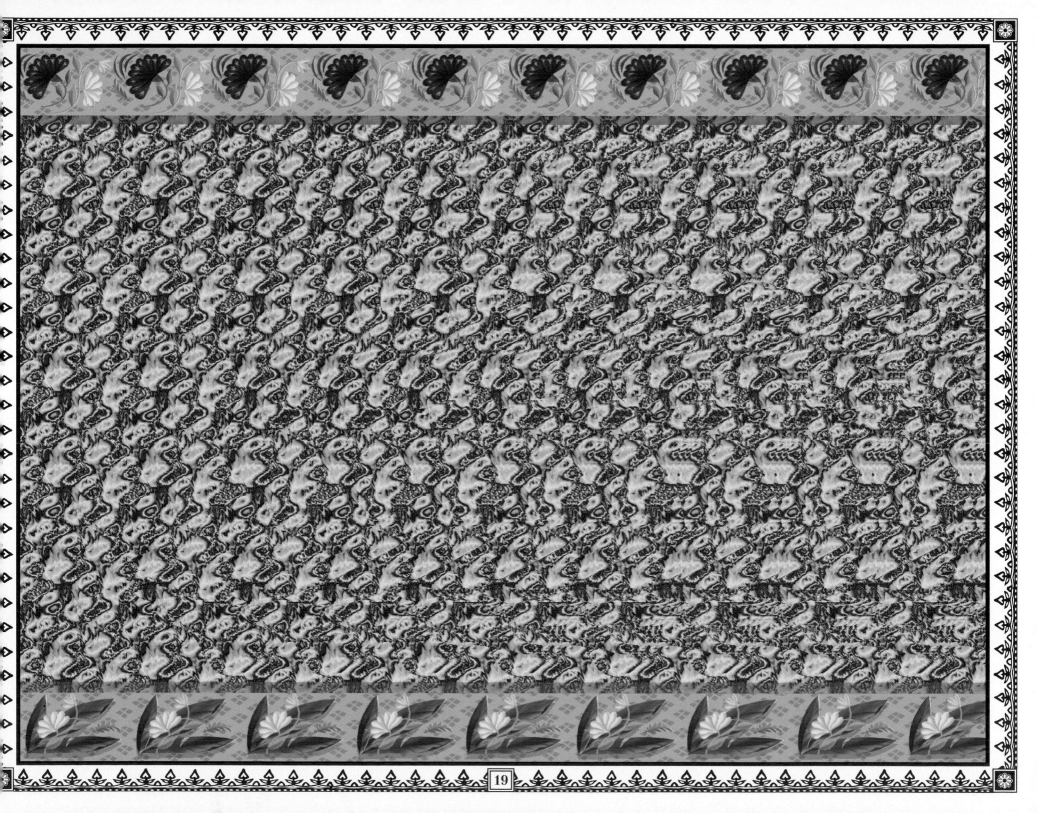

THE CURVING KNOT

The friends linger behind. One discusses the matters of love. The master of the house, however, thinks only of his beloved who awaits him. He thinks of the 'line of jewels' he left at the bottom of her back. This is what one calls a bite made with all of the teeth. One of the hosts recounts how he practises the curving knot position, which demands skill and suppleness. The master of the house smiles dreamily…Last night his beloved, as clever as a she-monkey, led him into this perilous exercise. His legs remember it still! Each partner puts their arms into the hollow of their knees and pulls their legs towards them. Holding each other's hands, yoni and lingam are brought closer. Reaching ecstasy in this delicate position is said to be a token of the lovers' eternal love.

THE DOG

U Unlike animals, the man presses his imagination into the service of love.

Like a god, he transforms as he pleases, as the whim takes him.

In accordance with his desires and those of his beauty, he turns into dog, fox, stag

or elephant. In comparison, none have seen a bull mount a cow as men do.

The beauty gets on all fours and, in that position, presents her rump which she

wiggles suggestively. If she claws the carpet, mews and purrs, it is the congress

of the cat. If she bleats and shakes her head violently, it is the assault of the goat.

If, with tears in her eyes, she wails, it is the rut of the stag.

If she groans, growls, licks her lover's fingers, then it is the union of the dog.

THE UNIFIED LOVERS

He expected to find her alone, but she is with her foster sister. He is not the kind of man to shirk his duty, but still! The naughty girls hardly allow him time to think. Before he knows what has hit him, he is in their arms. He must recognize them with his eyes closed. Which one kisses him? Which one scratches him? Whose yoni is this? He loses every time. His hands and his mouth are no match for the forfeits they impose. And now here are the two beauties, hip against hip, their legs raised, offering their yonis. Clasping them both in his arms, the seasoned lover switches from one to the other and, with all the valiance of his lingam, fills them with joy. It is the united congress.

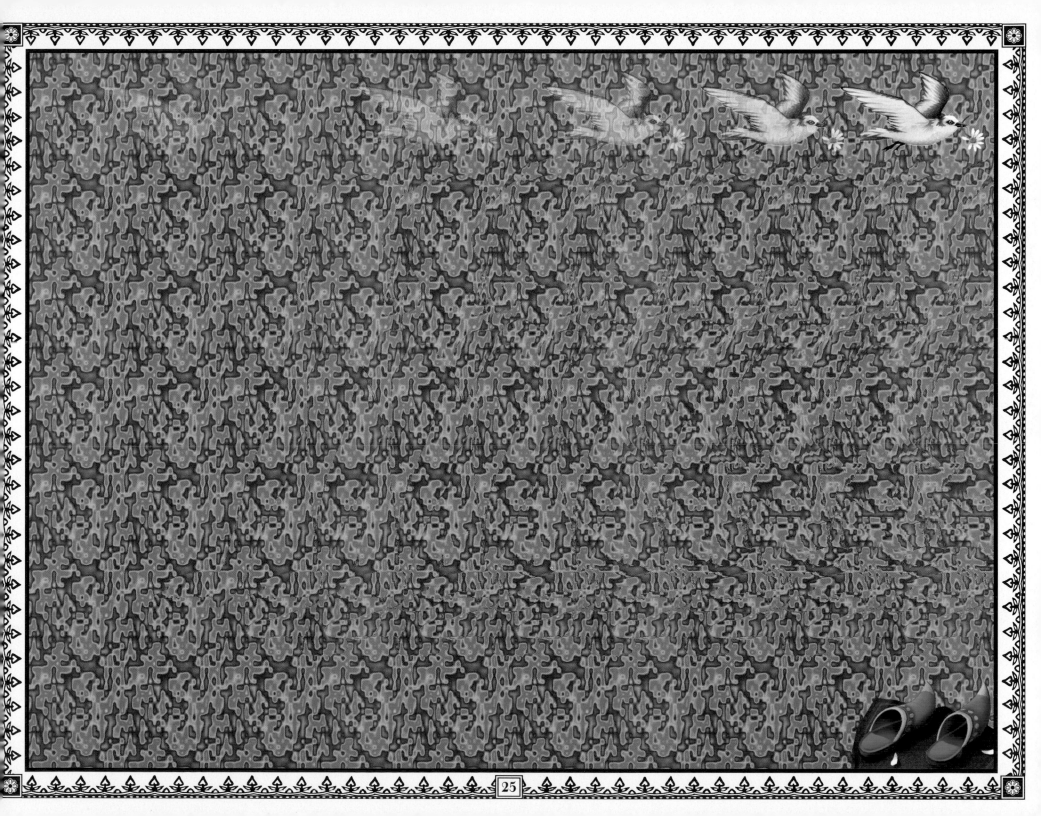

THE PESTLE

The room is perfumed, the flowered bed ready for love, but these two keep their distance, sulking. They are not lovers, they are deceived spouses. The unfaithful wife of one is attracted to the fickle husband of the other. They meet to talk it over. The betrayed wife sheds tears. The deceived husband is duty-bound to console her. How curious – he thought he did not like chubby women, yet this one arouses him endlessly. He wipes her cheek with a caress. Refusing to be indebted to such a nice man, she gives him a kiss. Rivalling each other in politeness, they cuddle, tickle, embrace. And now, clasping her in his arms, erect like a mast in the middle of the bed, he pounds her and polishes her. Delicious revenge.

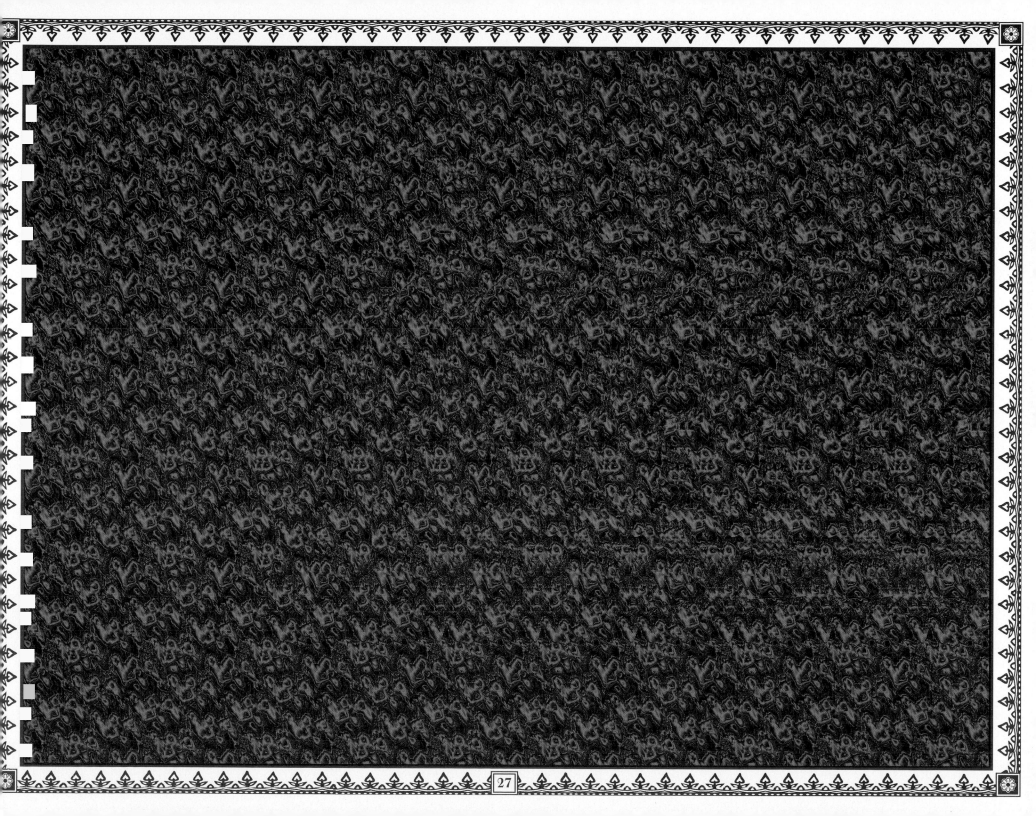

THE SPORTING OF A SPARROW

The young widow of a very old husband, she mourns for his tenderness and kindness. The river is grey. The flowers have lost their fragrance. Why was she stopped from throwing herself onto the pyre? She falls asleep. A tear rolls down her cheek, her sighs causing her lovely breasts to rise. Kama, the god without a body, is moved by this sight. He takes the shape of a handsome prince and lies down upon her. The perfume of jasmine mixes with the young man's musky odour. Brisk like a sparrow, the god's lingam goes back and forth continuously inside her yoni. She has never known anything like this with her husband. Her groans accompany the river's rumblings. The singing of the birds awakens her. Was it only a dream? Who would care! Today the mourning is over. She will go to the temple to make offerings to Kama, the god of all desires.

THE CHURNING OF THE CREAM

Kamadhenu, the celestial cow with the head of a woman, born from the churning of the Sea of Milk, has the gift of making every wish come true. The deserted wife prays to her. O Kamadhenu! She bemoans the happy times when her beloved showered her with caresses. And here is the lover returning! He had a dream, he says. Kamadhenu was before him. She had his beauty's face, her mouth was trembling, her beautiful eyes glistening with tears. Repentant, he throws himself to her knees. The lover forgives him. He embraces her, crushing her nearly to the point of suffocation. Hugs and kisses on her thighs, hugs and kisses on her breasts. Thanking the celestial cow for opening his eyes, the lover turns his lingam all around inside the delicious yoni. Divine reunion. Churning the cream.

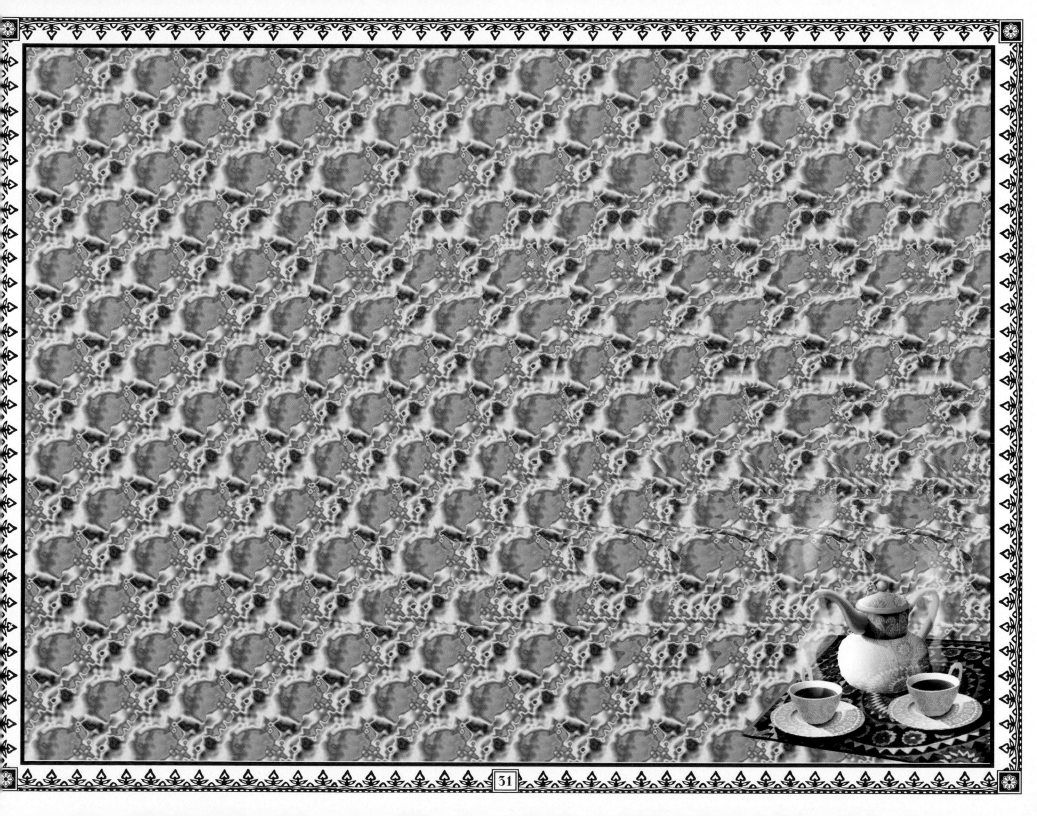

31

THE STAG

When he married her, she was a very young girl, almost a child. Now she is an accomplished woman, blessed with all the talents. They like to play and surprise each other. Today he finds her lying on the bed in the pleasure room. Her face is hidden by her splayed black hair. Slightly worried, he approaches. The wife has heard him and, with a swift move, she raises her rump. The fabrics fall away, revealing her superb buttocks. Without delay, savagely, like a stag in a rut, the husband mounts his wife. Suddenly, filled with scruples, he breaks off. Then the wife, with a move of her hip, encourages him and, in a dancing rhythm, she moves along with the back and forth motion of her man, who wails with pleasure.

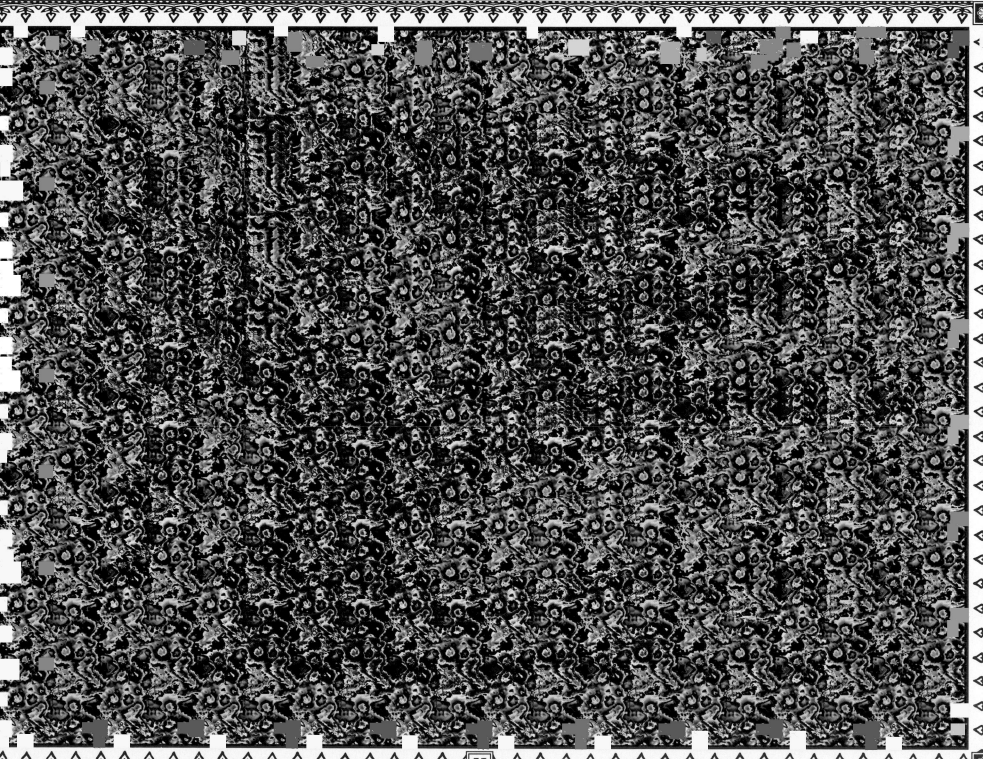

THE TIGRESS

A At last, the lover has returned. He has been away for a long time. The marks his embraces left on his beloved's body have long since faded. He is now intimidated as he faces his mistress. It appears as if these few weeks have transformed the beauty. He has never seen her so radiant. A doubt crosses his mind. Could she have deceived him? As if she had heard his jealous thoughts, the beauty digs her pearly nails into his shoulders. Tiger's claw, peacock's foot, leaf of a blue lotus, swollen bite, broken cloud, they use claws and teeth like wildcats. And then the cunning lover slides his hand between the beauty's thighs, caresses delicately the yoni, and turns the tigress into a purring and cuddly cat.

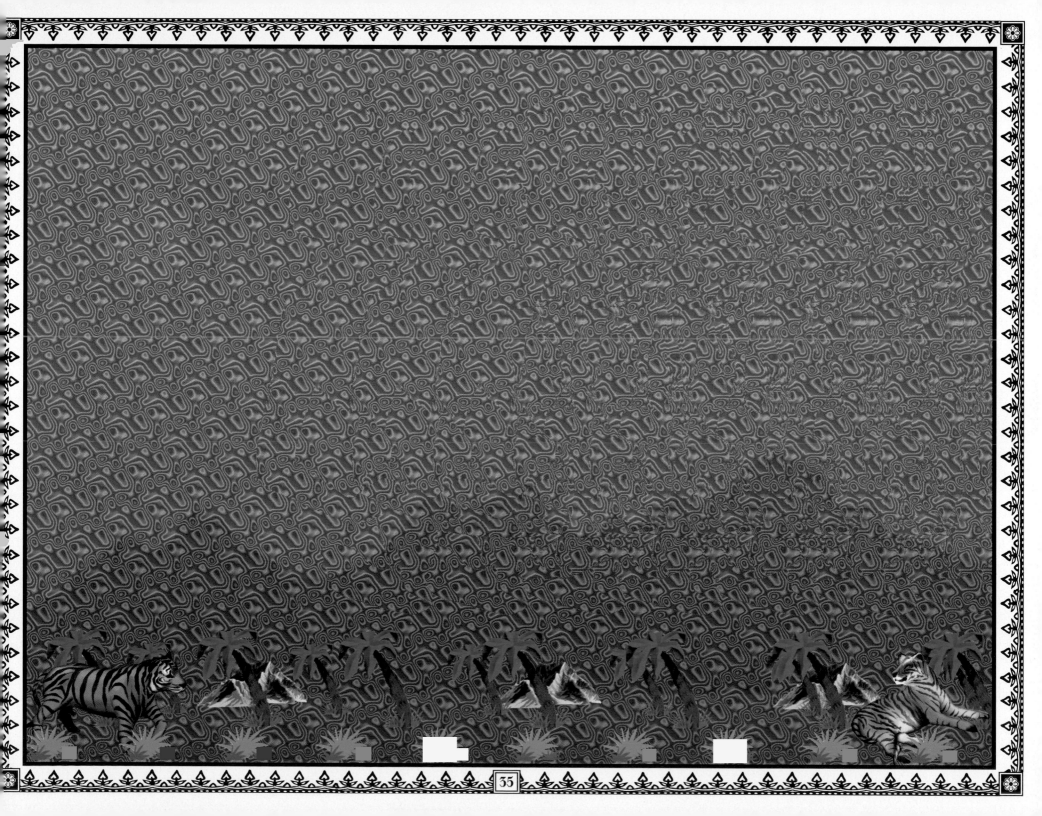

KNEE ELBOW

There are some lovers who despise soft beds and cosy cushions. Their pleasure is heightened by danger or discomfort. Some choose places where their union may be discovered; others practise the most hazardous positions. Others still seek risk and difficulty. Their pleasure room is a garden where they lay themselves open to being seen. The beauty, one foot on her lover's thigh, her arms hanging from his neck, coos as she lifts herself up his body. She looks like she's climbing a tree! Now she clasps her beloved's chest between her slender legs. She is now perched on his lingam. While she is moving up and down, held up by her lover's powerful arms, he whispers suggestive words in her ear.

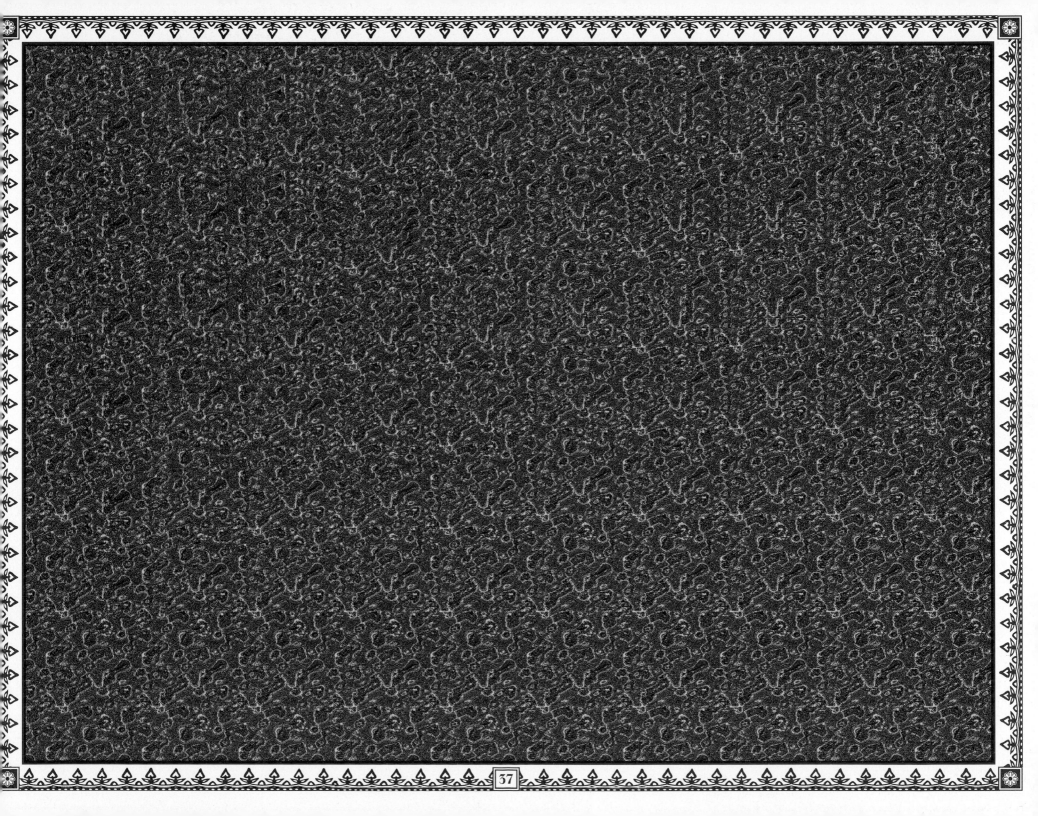

THE TRIPOD

The beautiful stranger has asked to visit the temple. And here she is, red with confusion, facing the friezes. On the walls all around her, human and divine creatures, with serene faces, make love in every fashion. Her guide, a handsome doe-eyed boy, shows her a small woman kissing the lingam of a man with the face of Buddha. She smiles dreamily. Taking her by the hand, the guide leads her into the temple's mazes. Here no one will disturb them. In an instant, they are as naked as the stone lovers. The tiles worn away by time do not make a welcoming bed! One of the beauty's legs rests on the young man's hip, he is going to love her while standing. She discovers unsuspected delights in this balanced love position.

INVERSION

The women of Maharashtra adore every kind of pleasure. The beautiful wife does not contradict this reputation. And, until dawn, she demands more from her husband. The poor man falls asleep…Never mind, she gives him a few betel leaves to chew, plies him with sweets, with fresh coconut milk. He can relax and she will take care of him. The husband lets himself drift. She rubs his body with a sandalwood unguent. Soon, the massages turn into caresses. The beauty excites his chest. He comes to and she mounts him. He would like to kiss her mouth but the naughty girl shies away, turns around, offering him her back. It is she who decides. She possesses him. Delicious submission.

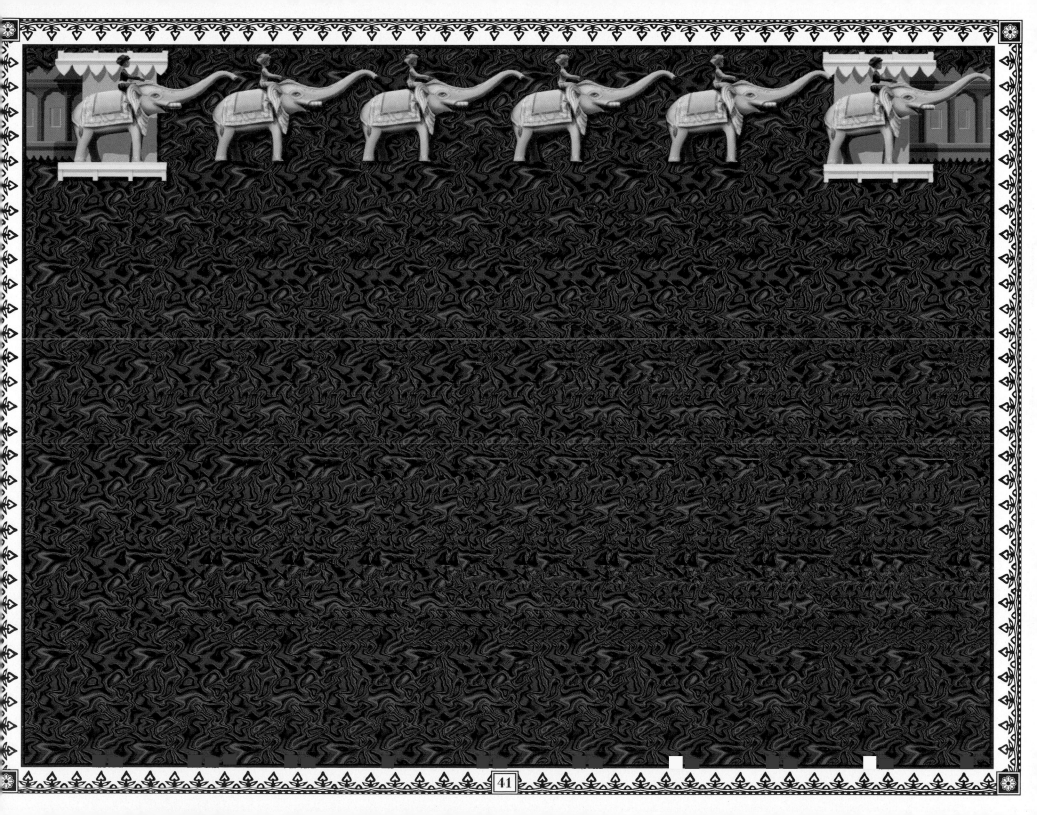

THE SHARPENING

Ardent young men, when you enter your mistress's yoni with your lingam, beware of spilling. By acting so grossly, you would leave her hungry for more. There are many ways in which a lingam shall behave with a yoni. Study your lover's reactions, read the look in her eyes. Because of her shyness, an inexperienced woman will not dare to express her desires. When you are in this situation, do not content yourself with merely pushing on. Any donkey can do that. Learn to break through by striking the upper part of the yoni, then by rubbing the lower part. Try the blow of a bull, the blow of a boar. Then you will see your lover, putting aside all bashfulness, cry out, lose her head and direct the love congress in the growing rhythm of her pleasure.

THE ELEPHANT

How can you fail to marvel at the elephant! So much strength combined with so much delicacy. See its trunk: powerful enough to uproot a tree, it can still embrace with grace, touch and skim with subtlety. Women are frightened and surprised by the size of the lingam. Men apply themselves to taming this mythical rival. The imaginative lover, however, does not care about rivals – men, women or beasts! He has no trunk, but it matters not! He embraces his beloved with his arms, lifts her up, turns her around. Inhaling her intoxicating perfumes, his mouth explores her body. His lingam strikes the beauty's thighs, caresses her yoni. She appreciates his vigour!

Today, for his lover's pleasure, he is Hastica the elephant.

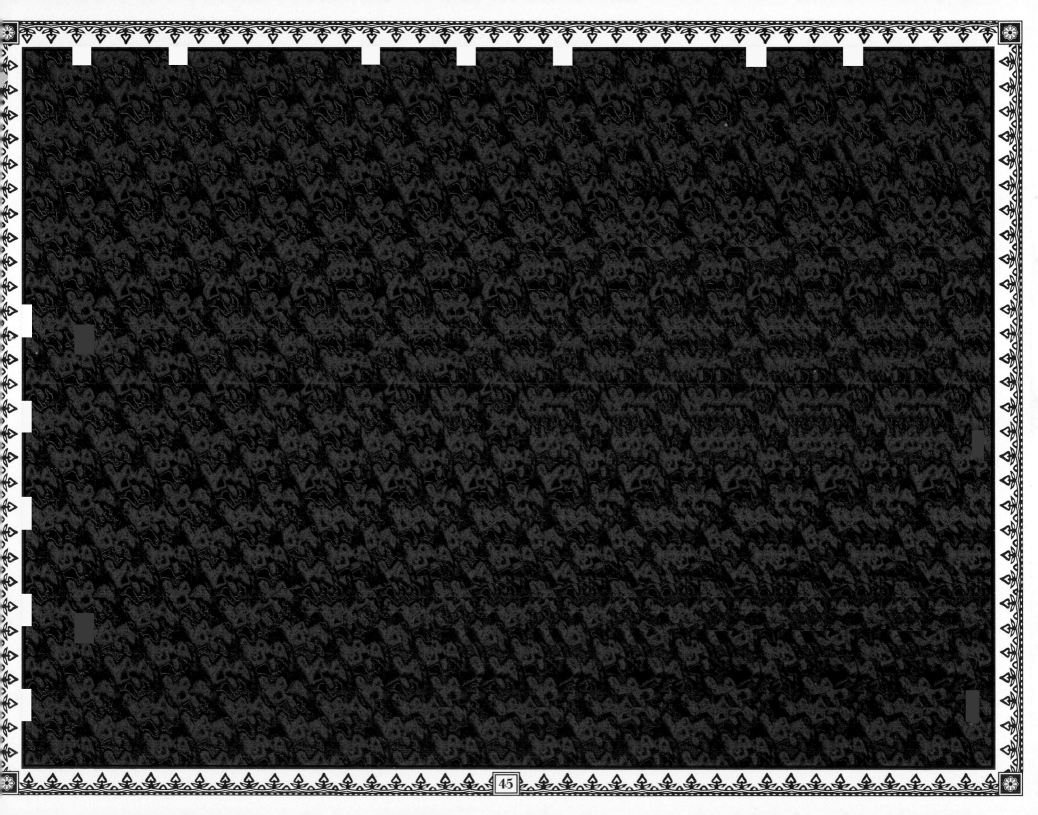

THE BLACK BEE

You no longer recognize your sweet love, this perfect and devoted wife. Is it the full moon? Today she resembles an Amazon. You sense that the proud warrior is ready to vanquish you and, offering her your belly like the wolf, you surrender. She mounts you, she is going to tame you. No use trying to resist. Her arrogant breasts, her flat belly, her strong and muscled thighs, her greedy mouth are so many weapons. Yours is here, modest but already up for the fight. The beauty grasps it. Sitting upon you, legs tucked up, she sucks your lingam into her yoni, until you cry out. Then – you did not know of such a hidden talent – she starts spinning like a top around your organ erected as a pivot.

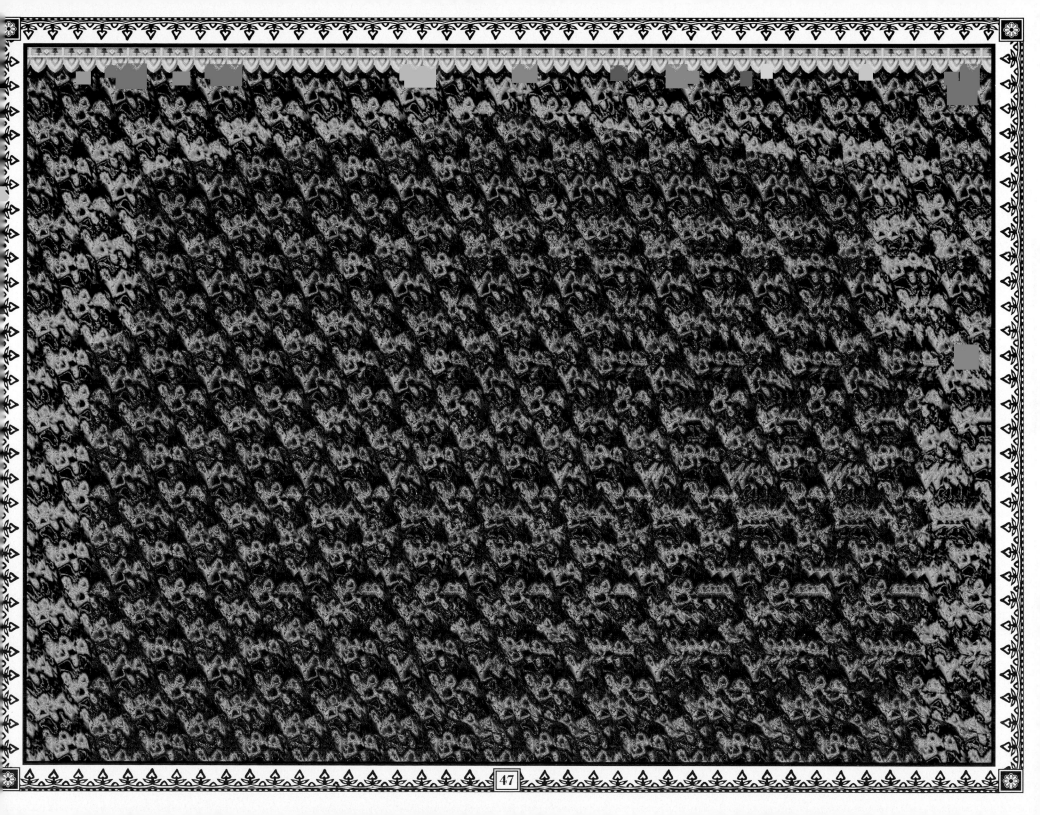

THE LOVEMAKING OF THE CROW

No place is as poorly guarded as a harem. And no women more accessible than the king's wives. A determined young man only has to choose how to achieve his ends. Hidden inside a barrel or disguised as a maidservant, he will easily deceive the casual sentinels and the overworked stewards. He can also try to make himself invisible by using an appropriate potion. But the result is uncertain. The king's wives like to play games with strangers that are forbidden with their husband. The young man and the noble lady are lying against each other, head to tail. He explores her yoni while her pretty mouth gobbles up his lingam greedily. It is Kalila the crow, the posture of slaves and maidservants, that queens are so fond of.

INDRANI

In ancient times darkness ruled. The gods, powerless against it, imagined and 'created' Indra. Indra the invincible killed the archdemon Vritra and, by so doing, allowed the organized world to triumph over chaos. Indra is beautiful like the sun. Like the sun, he is radiant. Only a 'Padmini', a perfect woman with one thousand qualities, can aspire to such a husband. But, as ancient authors claim, there is only one Padmini in ten million women. Still, the others need not despair! Through long and patient practice, any woman can perfect the position of Indrani, her legs tucked up, her feet resting on her thighs. Then she and her husband share a genuine encounter with the divine essence, token of fertility and love.

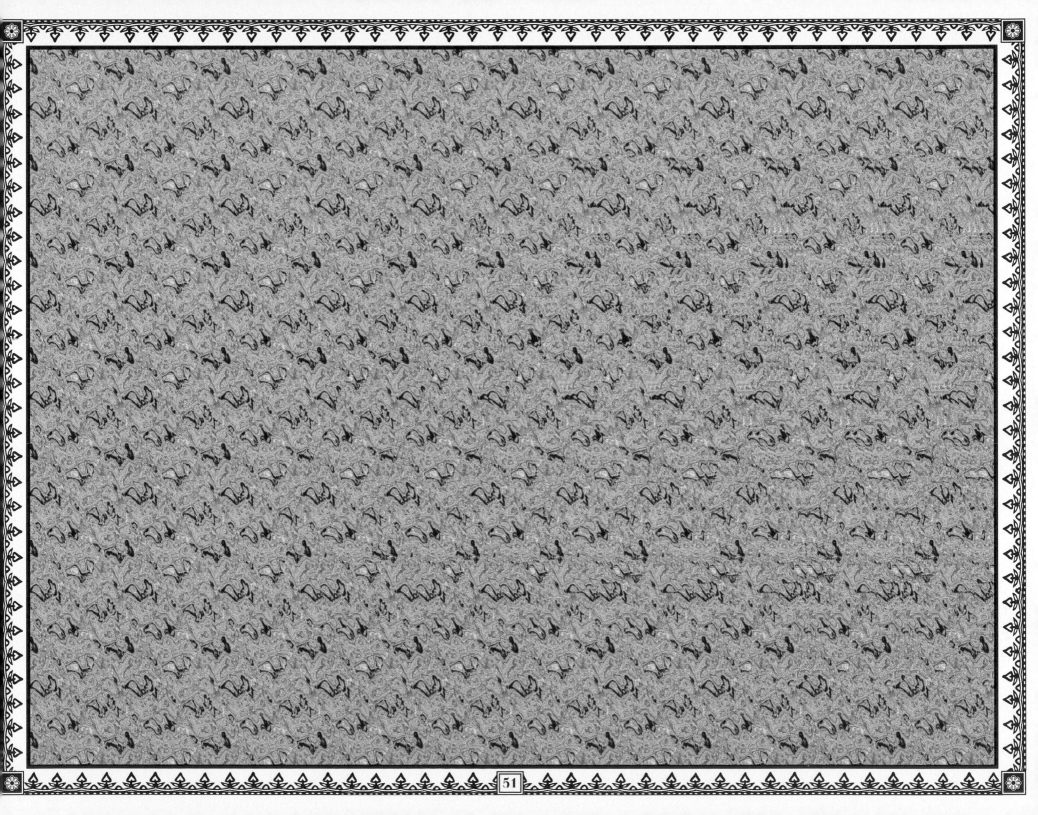

THE MARE

The reputation of the courtesan of the land of Andra is firmly established. She is said to make love with consummate artistry. It is also said that, unlike the mare, it is she who climbs astride her male. And when the lover is well in hand, tamed, saturated with caresses, she seizes his lingam. Deep inside her yoni, she squeezes it, strangles it: it is the blow of a mare. Men would like to own her. Women, too, and among them good wives who seek to perfect themselves in the art of love. But the courtesan of the land of Andra is not for sale. She is already rich enough. Today she is said not to have a lover. And all her love goes to Babu, her elephant.

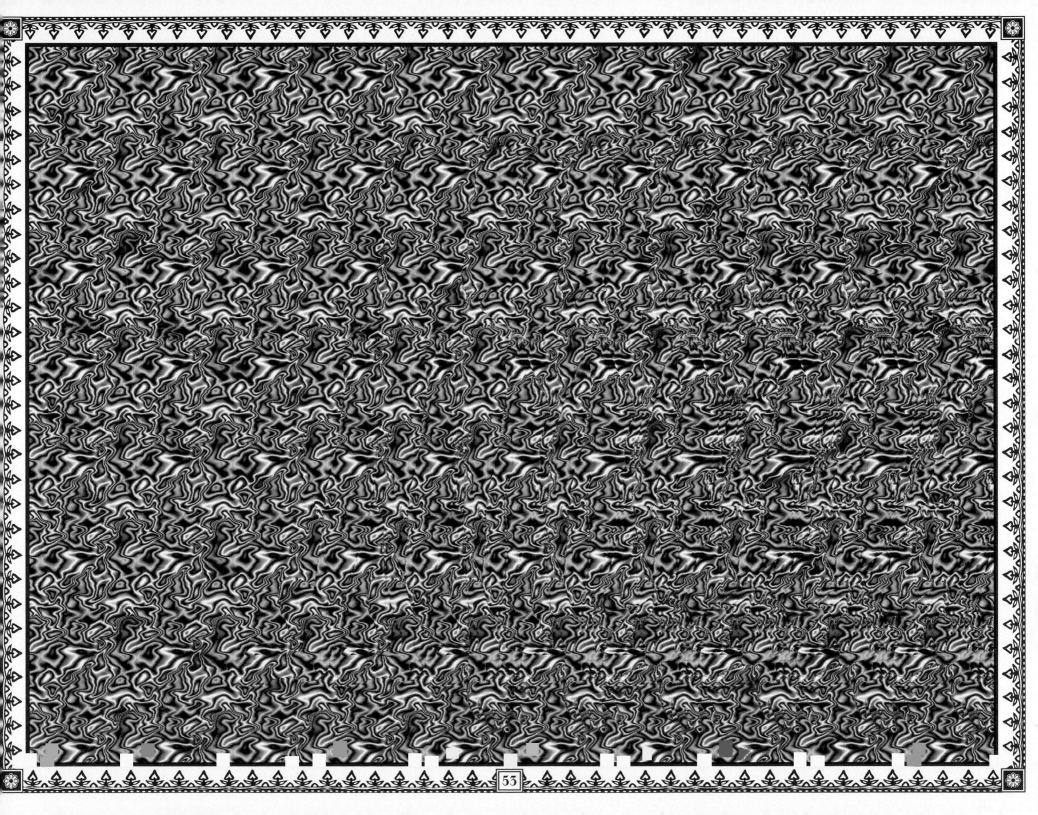

THE MIXTURE OF
SESAMUM SEED WITH RICE

L Lunch-time siesta, exhausting heat. Even the flies are sleeping.

Secretly, the engaged couple, shy and charming, meet. Straight kiss, bent kiss, turned kiss, pressed kiss, fighting tongues…They are well-mannered young people who have been taught the art of loving. But wait! Quick to forget the wise lessons, carried away by passion, they tear off, rip off the sweaty silk clothes which stick to their skin. They roll down on the cold, tiled floor like two young dogs. Mouth against mouth, gazing into each other's eyes, arms, thighs, legs tightly entwined…It is difficult to tell one from the other. The mixture of sesamum seed with rice. Lingam and yoni meet. The engaged couple have celebrated their wedding night prematurely!

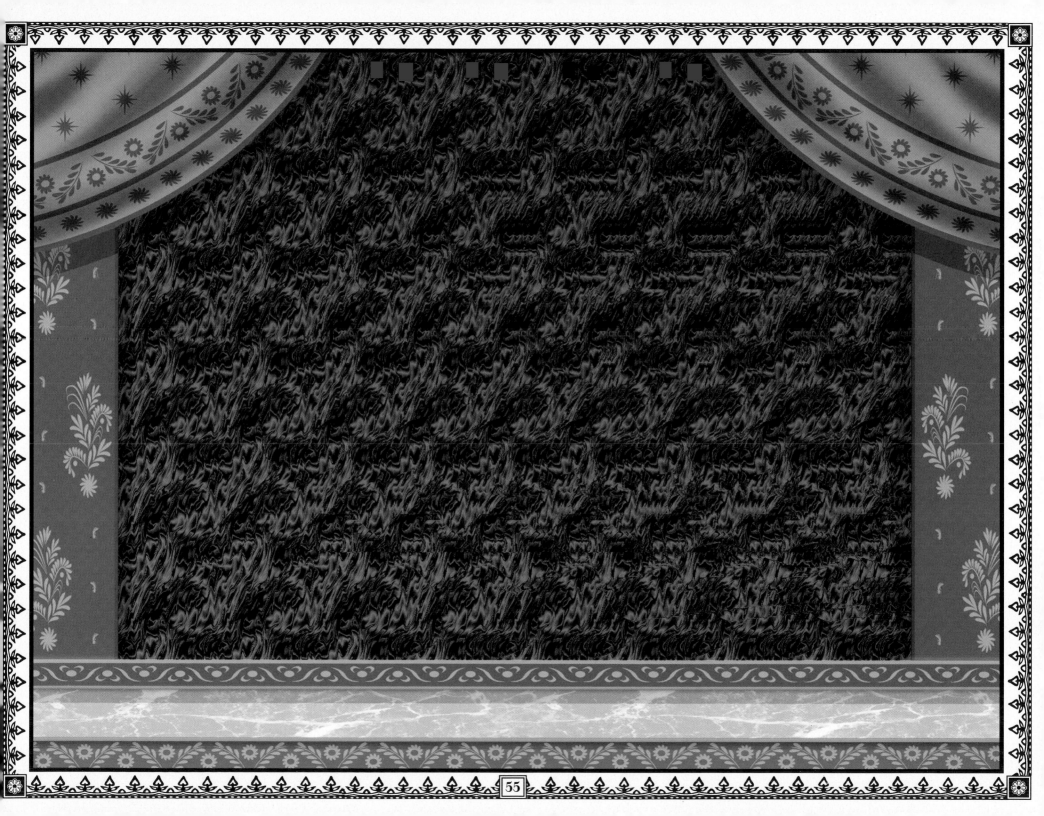

APADRAVYAS

Sometimes Kama, absent-minded, throws his arrow haphazardly. Thus one sees strange couples assembling. A man and a woman who should not have been brought together. They attract criticism, mockery. And yet, 'badly-matched' love defies time! This hare-man, thin and graceful, adores his elephant wife, as powerful as a giant. Their tastes, their preoccupations, like their bodies, are discordant. But they adore each other! And, in the games of love, their harmony is perfect. The hare-man knows all the subtle caresses that arouse his wife. Making use of Apadravyas, he increases the size of his frail lingam. There are all kinds of them in the pleasure room: gold armband, precious wood tube, ivory bracelet. They choose them according to how their lovemaking progresses.

SPLITTING THE BAMBOO

A charming scene: two young peasants singing under the moon. With the same slender figure, the same graceful gait, they look like the male and female forms of one single being. Their fresh voices chase the darkness away. They reach the river, at the spot named 'the bath of the goddesses'. Undressed in the twinkling of an eye, they dive…Now they lie down in the grass, fearless of snakes. Perched on top of a tree, Garuda, the bird of Vishnu, protects them. With the blessing of the sympathetic god, they soon become experts in the art of loving. With one leg stretched out along his slender body, the young girl puts her other leg on the boy's shoulder, then she inverses the legs' position, she alternates them.

It is splitting the bamboo. Celestial ballet!

THE PRELUDES
PAGE 11

THE YAWNING
PAGE 13

THE COBRA
PAGE 15

THE CONCH
PAGE 17

THE SWING
PAGE 19

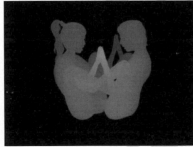

THE CURVING KNOT
PAGE 21

THE DOG
PAGE 23

THE UNIFIED LOVERS
PAGE 25

THE PESTLE
PAGE 27

THE SPORTING
OF A SPARROW
PAGE 29

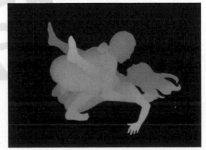

THE CHURNING
OF THE CREAM
PAGE 31

THE STAG
PAGE 33

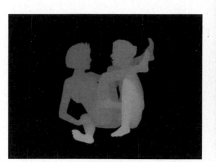

THE TIGRESS
PAGE 35

KNEE ELBOW
PAGE 37

THE TRIPOD
PAGE 39

INVERSION
PAGE 41

THE SHARPENING
PAGE 43

THE ELEPHANT
PAGE 45

THE BLACK BEE
PAGE 47

THE LOVEMAKING OF THE CROW
PAGE 49

INDRANI
PAGE 51

THE MARE
PAGE 53

THE MIXTURE OF
SESAMUM SEED WITH RICE
PAGE 55

APADRAVYAS
PAGE 57

SPLITTING THE BAMBOO
PAGE 59